Brewed with Fire and Faith

Daily Reflections from the Early Church

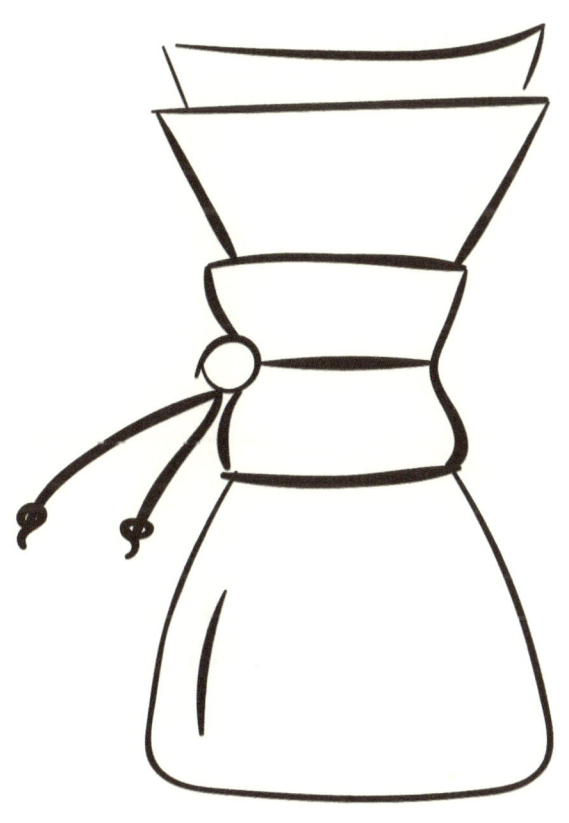

Brewed with Fire and Faith

Daily Reflections from the Early Church

Third Devotional in the
Coffee With The Preacher Series

Dr. Raymond Grabert, Jr.

To you who desire to know God
more-- May this devotional encourage
you to draw closer to Him!

May the stories of Acts deepen and
awaken your soul to His presence.

As you sit with a warm cup of coffee in
hand, may you find the comfort of the
Holy Spirit as you "Pour Over" His Word!

ALL FOR CHRIST!

Dr. Raymond
GRABERT

Table Of Contents

Notes

This manuscript was proofread and edited with the assistance of Chatgpt to identify grammatical errors, improve clarity, and ensure consistency. The manuscript was then proofread by Wanda Bowman for further identification of grammatical errors. All suggested edits were reviewed and finalized by the author, who remains responsible for the final content.

Introduction

I love stories. One of my fondest memories is of my Grandma Navarre telling stories about growing up on a plantation in South Louisiana. Looking back, I wish I'd had the foresight to record those stories for they have faded with time. Recording stories preserves both the memory of the person and the events they lived. The book of the Acts is filled with stories. Dr. Luke recorded these specific stories for a purpose and each tells something of God to us. As I wrote these devotions, I relived each story with joy as I discovered the wealth of inspiration God had waiting for me. May you discover for yourself the rich story God has for you in its pages. As you do, grab your Bible and your favorite study spot and engage God's Word. These devotions are designed to be cup-sized; short enough for a coffee break, yet thought-provoking enough to linger with you. Allow the Holy Spirit to speak to you as you read through Acts. Dwell on the importance of each story and allow Him to embolden your faith, stir your heart and enrich your mind. So, grab your cup of java and join me as we walk together through the Book of Acts.

All for Christ,

Dr. Raymond Grabert

Before You Begin

1. God's Word is most important! My words are just that, my words. Scripture always is primary in our lives.

2. Take your time. Do not rush the process! Read and reread God's Word. Allow It to saturate your heart and mind.

3. Remember, my words are just that, my words. These are my heart expressions when I read and meditated on God's Word.

4. Reflect along the way. Each devotion has a "Double Shot". Questions to guide your thoughts and apply that passage to your life.

5. The Gospel of Jesus Christ is our foundation.
- We are sinners under the condemnation of God's judgment. Romans 3:23
- Jesus gave His life to pay our sin debt. Romans 5:8
- God, through the sacrifice of Jesus, has given us life as a free gift. Romans 6:23
- We receive salvation when we place our faith and trust in the work of Jesus Christ on the cross on our behalf. Romans 10:13

Cup 1
Acts 1:1-11

"...you will be my witnesses in Jerusalem,..." vs 8b

Gone are the days of the Lone Ranger and Tonto riding in the Wild West as they fought bad guys. We looked up to them and found inspiration for living better lives. The book of Acts is the story of the Holy Spirit empowering men and women to transform their world. They transformed their world by inspiring and encouraging people to respond to the Good News of Jesus Christ. They had witnessed the resurrection of Jesus Christ and had received His command to share the Gospel. Their stories of inspiration live on motivating you to inspire others in your life. Jesus gave you the command to go and tell others. Mentor a new believer in Jesus. Teach a discipleship class. Get involved in a local congregation and become a model of what being a Christian is like to the upcoming generation. As you read through Acts, you will observe inspiring men and women of faith as they undertook the tremendous challenge of changing their world. May you be challenged as you hear afresh the command of Jesus to be a witness. Allow the Holy Spirit to empower you to share the Good News. Ask God to make you an inspiration to the next generation!

Double Shot

1. Who were a few of your heroes as a child?

2. How can I move from being a "lone ranger" Christian to an invested, engaged disciple mentoring a new believer, joining a discipleship group, or serving in my local congregation?

3. Take a moment and reflect upon your life. Who is someone who could benefit from being invested in?

Time For Prayer
Take a moment and communicate with God.

Cup 2
Acts 1:12-14

"They all were continually united in prayer, along with the women, including Mary the mother of Jesus, and his brothers." vs 14

Leaving a legacy is like the building of a great city, it is not built in a day. A legacy is built over time through habits, actions, attitudes and words. The Book of Acts draws attention to several men and women who left a legacy behind through how they lived and yet none of them intended to leave such a wonderful example behind. It all started in the upper room following Jesus' ascension. They gathered and there embarked on an action that would set the rest of their lives in motion. They PRAYED! Luke, the author of Acts, noted they were continually united in prayer together. They bathed the coming of the Holy Spirit and the rest of their lives in prayer. They sought God's guidance for what was next on their journey as disciples. Do you wish to leave a legacy that points others to Jesus? Spend time in prayer with God. What are the directions in your life which need adjusting? Which habits need to be removed and what habits need adding to help you leave behind that which really matters? Start your legacy on your knees!

Double Shot

1. Where do I need to slow down, seek God, and intentionally build habits that shape a Christ-centered legacy?

2. Which of my attitudes, actions, relationships, or hidden habits need to be surrendered to God in prayer so that He can realign them with His purposes?

3. How can I cultivate a rhythm of continual, united prayer that will guide my decisions and influence the legacy I desire to leave behind?

Time For Prayer:
Take a moment and communicate with God.

Cup 3
Acts 1:15-26

"Then they cast lots for them, and the lot fell to Matthias..." vs 26b

Setbacks are a part of living. Judas Iscariot is a name familiar to most people. His name is synonymous with betrayal. The disciples were crushed that one of their own had betrayed Jesus into the hands of the religious leaders who had Him crucified. This could have destroyed that little fragile group, but the resurrection brought unity instead. Looking to two Psalms (69:25, 109:8), Peter began leading the effort to replace Judas at the prompting of the Holy Spirit. You face setbacks in your life as well. A failed marriage, a financial disruption, or the passing of a loved one can bring disruptions in your life. Just as Peter trusted God's guidance to replace Judas, you too can rely on Him. Your trials do not have to cause you to stumble. You can move forward in the power of the Holy Spirit. Keep Jesus at the forefront of your life! Develop a deep appreciation for the salvation He has gifted you, and keep moving!

Double Shot

1. What recent setback in my life has the potential to discourage or derail me? How do I perceive God inviting me to trust His guidance in the midst of it?

2. Where do I need to surrender disappointment, grief, or confusion to the Holy Spirit so that He can turn what feels like a disruption into a place of renewal and forward movement?

3. How can I keep Jesus at the forefront of my thoughts, decisions, and reactions today so that my response to setbacks reflects the salvation and hope I have in Him?

Time For Prayer
Take a moment and communicate with God.

Cup 4
Acts 2:1-13

Then they were all filled with the Holy Spirit and began to speak in different tongues, as the Spirit enabled them." vs 4

The day of Pentecost is among the most important of days in Christianity. The coming of the Holy Spirit is so important to the individual believer because He is God with us. Jesus, the Son of God was "God with us" in the incarnation. God the Holy Spirit has taken the Son's place so we are never alone. Consider the impact He made on the day of Pentecost. He fulfilled the promise of Jesus for He came at the request of Jesus (John 14:16). No longer alone, the Holy Spirit was the presence of God they had experienced over the last several years. He empowered them to accomplish the impossible. They were empowered with boldness as they declared the Gospel message. No longer afraid, Peter stood with the other 11 and began to share. The importance of the Holy Spirit to us is reflected in the day of Pentecost. The Holy Spirit is still "God with us", He still empowers us to accomplish great tasks, and He still imparts courage to believers. May you not be afraid to embrace the Holy Spirit!

Double Shot

1. In what areas of my life do I most need to remember that the Holy Spirit is "God with me," present, active, and never leaving me alone?

2. Where do I need the Holy Spirit's empowerment to accomplish something that feels impossible in my own strength?

3. What situation or conversation is God inviting me to face with Spirit-given courage as Peter did on the day of Pentecost?

Time For Prayer
Take a moment and communicate with God.

Cup 5
Acts 2:14-36

"Peter stood up with the eleven, raised his voice, and proclaimed to them:" vs 14

Our lives are to be spent serving God. Though we have many different gifts and talents, we all have the same goal: the sharing of the Gospel. Peter's message to those listening to his first sermon was a clear demonstration of the Holy Spirit in his life. He assisted Peter in several ways. First, Peter spoke with courage, grounded in the reality of Jesus' resurrection, as he raised his voice to a great crowd of onlookers. Second, the Holy Spirit empowered him to address the people who were wondering if the disciples were drunk. Third, He gave Peter boldness to confront the crowd with their role in Jesus' death. When we embrace the power and presence of the Holy Spirit, He helps us share boldly, just as He did through Peter. We need encouragement, clarity, and extra boldness to speak with conviction about the grace of God. Whether we speak to one person or a thousand, we can be confident that God will guide us if we are speaking His truth. Fear does not have to hinder us. We can rely on the Holy Spirit as Peter did. How can you embrace the power of the Holy Spirit today to share God's grace?

Double Shot

1. What fears or insecurities most often prevent me from speaking about Jesus? How might the Holy Spirit be inviting me to rely on His courage instead of my own?

2. Where do I need the Spirit's clarity, boldness, or encouragement to faithfully share God's grace?

3. How can I embrace the Holy Spirit's presence so that my words, actions, and conversations point others to the truth of the Gospel?

Time For Prayer
Take a moment and communicate with God.

Cup 6
Acts 2:37-41

"that day about three thousand people were added to them." vs 41

One of the tenderest moments you can experience is the salvation of another person. When a person is convicted by the Holy Spirit, you have a front row seat to witness God change their hearts. You are given the privilege in that moment to see Ezekiel 36:26 played out. The experience is similar to witnessing the actual birth of a baby. The Gospel had been presented and the people were "pierced to the heart." Peter would go on and encourage repentance and faith in Jesus Christ. As a result, 3,000 people responded. After witnessing such a powerful move of God, Peter surely left that encounter eager to share the Good News again. Our own lives are bolstered and encouraged when we witness another person bowing and praying. Sharing becomes so much more enjoyable knowing that at any moment a person will be moved by God and enter the Kingdom. You must bear in mind that not all witnessing results in a person receiving Jesus, but sharing can result in seed planting or watering. Do not get discouraged. Do you want to witness this tender moment? Who can you share God's grace with so that you have the potential to witness a person repent and come to faith in Jesus Christ?

Double Shot

1. Who in my life might God be prompting me to share His grace with, trusting that the Holy Spirit can pierce their heart just as He did on the day of Pentecost?

2. How can I remain faithful in sharing the Gospel and allow God to use my words to plant or water seeds?

3. When was the last time I witnessed God working in someone's life, and how can I let that memory rekindle my passion and eagerness to share the Good News again?

Time For Prayer
Take a moment and communicate with God.

Cup 7
Acts 2:42-47

"They ate their food with joyful and sincere hearts." vs 46b

Community life is one theme of the Book of Acts. Our life in the Kingdom of God is a major concern for Luke as he recounts the early church's movements. From the very beginning, the church shared life together. You need other believers, you need the church! Many see the church as outdated or irrelevant. Such thinking is a deception of the enemy for you need one another for encouragement and discipleship. Early on, the church gathered for the purpose of increased knowledge about Jesus. Knowing more about Jesus led to an increase of fellowship where meals were shared and most importantly, prayer. The result of their congregating together was spiritual growth. Luke observed that "everyone was filled with awe." Having others who had been impacted by the Gospel encouraged them. Do you wish to experience the same connection as those early believers? If you have a home church, be faithful to worship and gather. Experience afresh the blessings of joy, growth, encouragement, love and connection. If you do not have a church home, seek one out and discover the community God wishes for you!

Double Shot

1. In what ways am I actively engaging in community life with other believers, and what might be holding me back from deeper fellowship?

2. How has gathering with other Christians helped me grow spiritually, and where do I sense God calling me to be more faithful or intentional?

3. If I am not currently connected to a church community, what steps can I take this week to seek out a home church where I can experience the joy, encouragement, and growth described in Acts?

Time For Prayer
Take a moment and communicate with God.

Cup 8
Acts 3:1-10

"I don't have silver or gold, but what I do have, I give you..." vs 6

Peter and John were not wealthy men. Silver and gold were not theirs in abundance, but they did go around with Jesus in their hearts. If they considered ministry by their wealth, the lame man would have stayed lame. When he cried out for assistance that day, little did he know he was going to receive more than a silver coin. Empowered by the Holy Spirit, Peter and John offered physical healing which was greater than money. Like Peter and John, you are called to adopt a ministry mind-set: not one based on material resources, but on a relationship with Jesus. Many do not reach out to others in need because we feel inadequate. Sometimes you allow a sense of inadequacy to hold you back, but God invites you to trust that He has already equipped you. Peter and John overcame this by honestly evaluating their lack, "I don't have silver or gold, but what I do have, I give you...". Jesus does not ask you to give what you do not have. You already possess all you need to minister in His name. Spend time reflecting on excuses made in the past. Ask God to give you a fresh view of your ability in Jesus to reach out.

Double Shot

1. What are some areas in my life where I have felt inadequate to serve others, and how can I shift my focus from what I lack to what I already have in Jesus?

2. In what practical ways can I begin to minister to others, not by relying on material resources, but by sharing the love and power of Jesus that I already possess?

3. How has God equipped me, despite my perceived limitations, to be a blessing to someone else? What steps can I take today to step out in faith and offer what I have to those in need?

Time For Prayer
Take a moment and communicate with God.

Cup 9
Acts 3:11-26

"When Peter saw this, he addressed the people:"vs 12

There is an old saying, "When life gives you lemons, make lemonade." The saying encourages you to make the best of your life. Peter certainly did this when he took advantage of his situation to present the Gospel after the healing of the lame man. The moment was right for an explanation as to what happened. When you are given an opportunity, speak up for Jesus and share the Good News. Some opportunities are obvious to you such as people asking you how you maintained control of your car when the tire blew out. Others can quietly drift our way and are very subtle. The wise disciple develops discernment and wisdom to recognize opportunities. You can be like Peter and take advantage of any given situation and deliver a comprehensive presentation of the Gospel. Your presentation should also be as complete as possible. Be aware of the opportunities at hand, be brave and fight the fear of sharing, and be quick to tell others about Jesus.

Double Shot

1. How attentive am I to the subtle moments God places in my path, and what can I do to cultivate the kind of spiritual discernment that recognizes an opportunity to speak about Jesus?

2. What fears or hesitations most often keep me silent when the door opens for me to share the Good News, and how might God be inviting me to trust Him more boldly in those moments?

3. When God provides an opportunity to speak about my faith, how can I prepare my heart and mind so that my response is clear, complete, and centered on the Gospel?

Time For Prayer
Take a moment and communicate with God.

Cup 10
Acts 4:1-4

"They were annoyed that they were teaching the people and proclaiming in Jesus the resurrection of the dead." vs 2

Responses to the Gospel are as varied as the people we encounter. Some will believe and some will reject the message. We will be wise to consider that not all people will be happy when they are exposed to the truth of God. Our spiritual problem requires humility, but even more, it requires faith in Jesus, the only true solution. Our society does not accept such solutions as humility of heart. Jesus warned His disciples to anticipate rejections and persecutions. Sometimes rejection comes quietly, some simply decline to engage. Other times it is more intense. Peter and John were sharing the story of Jesus and ended up arrested. The religious leaders were hostile toward them. They did not want to acknowledge the truth that Jesus was the long-awaited Messiah. Do not be shocked if your best friend or favorite aunt does not want to talk about spiritual issues with you. Do not be afraid if others become defensive or even hostile when you speak truth. Stand firm in your faith and remember that, as verse 4 says, "many of those who heard the message believed."

Double Shot

1. How do I typically respond when someone rejects or resists the Gospel, and what does my reaction reveal about my trust in Jesus and His work in their heart?

2. In what ways can I prepare myself—spiritually and emotionally—to stand firm in my faith when conversations about Jesus are met with discomfort, defensiveness, or hostility?

3. Who in my life may need to hear the truth with patience and humility from me, and how can I remain faithful in sharing Christ even when responses are unpredictable or discouraging?

Time For Prayer
Take a moment and communicate with God.

Cup 11
Acts 4:5-12

"Let it be known to all of you and to all the people of Israel, that by the name of Jesus Christ of Nazareth. . . By him this man is standing here."

vs 11

Who you are is revealed by what you say and do. Peter and John were asked to give the reason for why and how they healed a crippled man. The moment was perfect to boast in their ability to heal! They could have taken all of the credit, but that was not who they were. Peter allowed the Holy Spirit to guide his words and took advantage of the audience to reveal the person who had radically changed his life, Jesus! Instead of taking the center of attention, all eyes were turned to the wonderful message of the Gospel. He highlighted in quick fashion the Good News. An individual who has experienced Jesus cannot help but speak of Him and His wonderful work. Have you experienced the transforming power of Jesus Christ? Do you then desire to share that transformation with others? Ask God to help you discern the right moment in your conversations to share your faith as Peter and John. Live out who you are in Jesus and point to Him.

Double Shot

1. When people listen to my words and watch my actions, do they see someone pointing to Jesus or someone seeking attention for themselves?

2. How has Jesus changed my life in a way that naturally leads me to speak of Him?

3. Am I willing to ask God for the courage and discernment to recognize those moments in everyday conversations when I can lift up the name of Jesus?

Time For Prayer
Take a moment and communicate with God.

Cup 12
Acts 4:13-22

"When they observed the boldness of Peter and John...recognized they had been with Jesus." v. 13

Peter and John had caused a stir when they healed the lame man. The religious leaders were upset that they were teaching about Jesus Christ. Noting their background, the leaders recognized something familiar. Their mannerisms and responses to their questions revealed a deeper connection to Jesus than just a surface claim. Conduct is a direct reflection of our spiritual inner reality as Jesus taught, "what comes out of the mouth comes from the heart".(Matthew 15:18) There is a certain intentionality in how we live that makes you stand out from the rest of the world. You intentionally make peace, intentionally use kind words, and intentionally seek righteousness. These are actions which are Holy Spirit driven as Peter and John responded, "we are unable to stop speaking about what we have seen and heard." Your actions and words betray whether you are a disciple of Jesus Christ or not. Take a moment and evaluate your life. How have your words and actions over the last few days reflected Jesus being lived out. Do your words betray a heart touched by Jesus or self? What do your words and actions reveal?

Double Shot

1. When others observe my words and actions, do they recognize something in me that points back to having been with Jesus?

2. In the past few days, where have I intentionally chosen peace, kindness, and righteousness, and where have I allowed my old self to speak instead?

3. If my conduct is a window into my heart, what does it reveal about who is truly shaping my inner life?

Time For Prayer
Take a moment and communicate with God.

Cup 13
Acts 4:23-34

"And now, Lord, consider their threats, and grant that your servants may speak Your word with all boldness." v. 29

Jesus taught that the world we live in will not accept us because it did not accept Him. Peter and John's opposition could have caused a deep disruption of life in the early church. The early group quickly turned to prayer. Their prayers resulted in a deepening dependence upon God for strength. The first result: a mighty move of the Holy Spirit as God confirmed His presence in their lives. The second result: they were further bound together in Jesus. They were together in "one heart and mind". The third result: an increase in boldness to testify of Jesus Christ. They would tell of Jesus regardless of the cost. The last result: a unified sharing of life. They shared their lives as needs were met among them. You do not have to be hindered by opposition as a believer. Consider how you respond when opposition comes your way. Spend time in prayer now and ask God for the same boldness in your life as He instilled in those early believers.

Double Shot

1. When I face opposition for my faith, do I instinctively turn to God in prayer as the early believers did, or do I rely on my own strength?

2. How is God calling me to walk in deeper unity and boldness with other believers, especially when pressure or resistance comes?

3. In what ways can I share my life more fully with others in the body of Christ so that needs are met and Jesus is honored?

Time For Prayer
Take a moment and communicate with God.

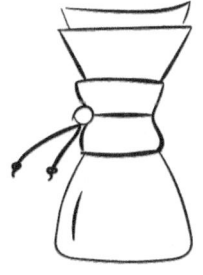

Cup 14
Acts 4:32-37

"This was distributed to each person as any had need." v. 35

The life of a believer is lived in community with others. Shared experiences of salvation bound the early believers. The church was more than a wonderful place where a multitude of different personalities gathered and worshiped. It was a place where the Holy Spirit gathered various men and women who had found eternal life in Jesus could openly live out their faith. Jesus was the common denominator that bound them together and motivated ministry one to another. When one was in need, they came together to help. When one was hurt, they gathered and provided comfort and relief. They laughed, cried, and loved together. So powerful was their connection that, "there was not a needy person among them because all those who owned lands or houses sold them". The disciples then distributed those funds to fill the needs. The church is a great place to gather, identify, and live life! No other reason to join a church is needed. The church is the place to live out our faith! Where do you live out your faith? Have you identified with other like-minded believers and joined them? Ask God to guide you to the church He would have you live out your faith.

Double Shot

1. How am I actively living out my faith within a community of believers rather than trying to walk the Christian life on my own?

2. In what ways am I sharing life with others so that I can help, encourage, and support them as the early church did?

3. Have I sought out the church family God desires for me, and am I willing to let Him guide me into deeper connection and commitment?

Time For Prayer
Take a moment and communicate with God.

Cup 15
Acts 5:1-11

"Why did you agree to test the Spirit of the Lord?" v. 9

Belonging to God's Kingdom, the Church, is a privilege. One's actions within the Church are vital to its growth, maturity, and success. Remember the Church is not the building but the people. For this reason, the passage under consideration takes on significance. Ananias and Sapphira's story highlights the importance of each person in the church. You will either live a righteous or unrighteous life. When you live for Jesus and strive to obey His righteous standards, the Church grows and becomes what He desires. If you live an unrighteous life, you negatively impact the church. Your actions are seen as being characteristic of the whole. The world looks at the cracks in the individual members and then transfers that unholiness onto others who are striving to be holy. The early church learned a valuable lesson the day Ananias and Sapphira learned not to lie to God the Holy Spirit. How you live greatly matters. What picture do outsiders see portrayed from your life? Repent of unrighteousness in your life and turn to God. Allow Him to use your life to be a picture of righteousness to an outside world. How you live matters!

Double Shot

1. What picture of the Church do my words and actions paint for those who are watching from the outside?

2. Are there attitudes or behaviors in my life that weaken the witness of Christ's people and need to be brought to God in repentance?

3. How can I intentionally allow the Holy Spirit to shape my daily conduct so that my life reflects the righteousness Jesus desires for His Church?

Time For Prayer
Take a moment and communicate with God.

Cup 16
Acts 5:12-16

"Many signs and wonders were being done among the people through the hands of the apostles." v. 12

The early church was a very attractive place as outsiders recognized a might move of God. Acts 5:15 notes the extent people went to in order to find healing. Even to the extreme of just desiring "at least his (Peter's) shadow might fall on them".Outsiders viewed them as a group which had a great testimony: healing could be found. As a result, the Gospel was given serious consideration and Luke notes that a great number of people started following Jesus Christ. This brings up a serious consideration for the modern Christian. Do people on the outside of the Kingdom of God see the church as a place where healing occurs? Have people stopped coming to church because transformation of lives has stopped? Serious consideration must be given to this matter. The church is to be the place where the sickness of sin and death can be addressed in such a manner that healing of the soul takes place. Jesus still desires to heal men and women. He still desires to transform sinful lives into righteous lives and the church is to be the proclaimer of that message. So, is the church, where healing takes place?

Double Shot

1. When people outside the Kingdom look at my church, do they see a place where genuine healing and transformation still take place?

2. Has my own life reflected the kind of change that would cause others to take the Gospel seriously, or have I grown silent about what Jesus can do?

3. How can I pray, serve, and live in such a way that my church becomes a clearer witness of the healing Jesus still desires to bring?

Time For Prayer
Take a moment and communicate with God.

Cup 17
Acts 5:17-21a

"Go and stand in the temple, and tell the people all about this life." v. 20

The disciples found themselves arrested for sharing the Good News of Jesus Christ. The temptation would be to reconsider their purpose in life and make changes to simply go with the flow. Early morning light would witness God releasing His disciples and commanding them to continue proclaiming! Guess what they did? They were obedient! The disciples walked out of prison and immediately began teaching people in the temple about Jesus. Some today are tempted to say, "I have never been told of God's purpose for my life as a believer!" Consider Matthew 28:18-20. Read this passage and recognize that what is called the "Great Commission" is for all believers. Jesus' purpose for all of His followers is for them to tell the whole world the story of the Gospel(Good News). Your purpose is the same as the disciples in this Cup's passage...evangelism. Go and accomplish God's purpose! Have you been faithful to obey God's command to share the Good News of Jesus? Take time and share Jesus with someone in your life this week.

Double Shot

1. When God clearly calls me to speak about Jesus, do I obey, or do I shrink back and "go with the flow"?

2. How seriously am I taking the Great Commission in my own life, knowing that Jesus has already given every believer a clear purpose?

3. Who in my life needs to hear the Good News this week, and will I be faithful to share Jesus with them?

Time For Prayer
Take a moment and communicate with God.

Cup 18
Acts 5:21b-32

"We must obey God rather than people." v. 29

Peter and the other disciples have moved from being timid to fearless in a short amount of time! A boldness had emerged and was evident as they declared, "We must obey God rather than people". The religious leaders took them to task over preaching and teaching the Good News of Jesus. Peter stood firm in the power of the Holy Spirit and expressed his personal conviction about Jesus Christ. The disciples could not back down or quit talking about Jesus because of what they had experienced firsthand (v. 32). They lived with Jesus and witnessed the miracles and heard His teachings. They were convinced He was the long-awaited Messiah. Stemming from their experience was their understanding of how they were to live. They could do nothing less than be obedient to God. Are you like the early disciples? Do you live by a conviction that Jesus is the Messiah? Reflect upon your relationship with God the Father. Does your relationship give you strength of conviction to declare as the disciples did, "I must obey God?"

Double Shot

1. In what areas of my life do I feel timid or hesitant about my faith, and what might God be inviting me to surrender so that I can live with the same Spirit-empowered boldness the disciples displayed?

2. What specific step of obedience is God calling me to take that would demonstrate my conviction that Jesus truly is the Messiah?

3. How does my daily relationship with God strengthen my ability to say, "I must obey God," even when obedience is difficult or unpopular?

Time For Prayer
Take a moment and communicate with God.

Cup 19
Acts 5:33-42

"they went out. . .rejoicing that they were counted worthy to be treated shamefully on behalf of the Name." v. 41

The disciples counted it a joy to have been found worthy of experiencing a beating for preaching in the name of Jesus Christ. Their encounter with Jesus Christ radically transformed them into men of conviction. So convinced that Jesus was the Messiah they stood firm, even in the face of physical assault. They suffered as Jesus suffered, and their response reflected His (John 19:1). The disciples did not cave but remained resolute in their convictions. They even considered it a privilege to have been beaten for being a follower of Jesus. Reflect a moment on how you might respond compared to the early disciples. They counted it a joy, would you count it a joy or feel too much pressure to be accepted in place of rejection? Persecution seems to create a fear that quiets voices. Could you experience a difficult response to the Gospel with a feeling of joy? Would you be willing to be fired from your job for being a Christian and to have a joyful attitude following it? Could you be like the disciples and rejoice that you would be counted worthy of being treated shamefully?

Double Shot

1. When I imagine facing rejection, criticism, or loss because of my faith, what emotions surface in me, and what do those emotions reveal about the depth of my conviction in Christ?

2. If obedience to Jesus cost me something significant, how would I choose to respond, and what practices can I begin now that would strengthen my resolve to remain faithful?

3. How can I cultivate such closeness with Christ that I could view suffering for His name not as a setback but as a privilege that draws me deeper into His heart and His mission?

Time For Prayer
Take a moment and communicate with God.

Cup 20
Acts 6:1-7

"There arose a complaint by the Hellenistic jews against the Hebraic Jews" v. 1

Struggles in life are a common occurrence. Additional daily ministry tasks became overwhelming and more than the disciples could handle. The disciples faced the truth of their struggles when they declared, "It would not be right for us to give up preaching the word of God to wait on tables". Keeping focused on what really mattered, the disciples sought a solution. The disciples and the early congregation developed a solution. Together, the wonderful ministry arm of the Church came into being — Deacons! Struggles are not necessarily bad, God can use those moments for your good (Romans 8:28). You can actually experience growth when you stop seeing struggles as evil and bad. Note the end result: further growth of the church. Are you going through a hard or difficult time? Do not view it as a bad thing to run from and avoid. Stop for a moment, take a deep breath, and view it as an opportunity for personal growth. God wants to grow you physically, emotionally, and spiritually. What struggle could you embrace and trust God to use for your growth and His glory?

Double Shot

1. Are you walking through a struggle right now that feels like more than you can manage? Have you taken a moment to honestly admit the weight of it instead of trying to push through on your own?

2. What difficult situation in your life could you stop running from and begin to see as an opportunity for growth? What step could you take today to lean into that struggle and allow God to use it for your good?

3. How might God be inviting you to trust that He is working Romans 8:28 in your life? In what way can you surrender this struggle to Him and believe He will use it to grow you physically, emotionally, and spiritually—for His glory?

Time For Prayer
Take a moment and communicate with God.

Cup 21
Acts 6:8-15

"And all who were sitting in the Sanhedrin looked intently at him and saw that his face was like the face of an angel." v.15

Do you reflect the light of Jesus? Stephen was one of the first deacons. He was a godly man who walked by the Holy Spirit. Anyone crossing paths with this man recognized his devotion to Jesus Christ. Even when his godly worldview collided with the Jewish religious leaders and he faced persecution, he refused to back down. Though he was brought before the Sanhedrin on false charges, he never responded with anger or hate. As he stood accused, the Holy Spirit's presence shone through his face, just as Moses' face reflected God in Exodus 34:29-35. Because he allowed the Holy Spirit to guide his heart, his words and his actions, these reflected a deep relationship with God. Stephen is a great example of a believer who took a bold stand and allowed God to be given glory through his life. Take a moment and reflect on whether others can see the light of Jesus shining through you. Do you obey God's commands to the point that the Holy Spirit shines through your life? Your relationship with God shines through your words, actions, and life when you surrender unto Him.

Double Shot

1. When others cross my path, do they sense the presence of Jesus in me the way people did with Stephen, or are there attitudes and reactions in my life that dim the light God wants to shine through me?

2. In moments when my faith collides with opposition or misunderstanding, how do I typically respond? What would it look like for me to allow the Holy Spirit to guide my words, actions, and attitudes instead?

3. What area of my life needs deeper surrender so the Holy Spirit can shine through me more clearly?

Time For Prayer
Take a moment and communicate with God.

Cup 22
Acts 7:1-60

"He knelt down and cried out with a loud voice, Lord, do not hold this sin against them! And after saying this, he died" v. 60b

One word surfaces with Stephen's last sermon — Continuity! Stephen recounts God's wonderful story. His message started in Genesis with Abraham and ended with Jesus. Stephen's point was God is actively involved in human history from times past to times yet to come. God is not passive, He takes an active interest in the affairs of mankind. You can find comfort in knowing that your life is in His sights right now. Nothing happens to you that He is not aware of. Stephen's own death unfolds in the eyes of God. Verses 55 and 56 reflect God's knowledge of what was happening as Stephen looks up and sees God the Son (Jesus) at the right hand of God the Father. The man he was in life is the same at the time of his death. He models how you can die, assured that even in death, God knows and is present. Continue to trust in God no matter what your future holds, He is already there.

Double Shot

1. Do I live each day with the assurance that God is actively involved in my story, or do I sometimes fall into thinking He's distant or unaware of what I'm walking through?

2. How would my response to uncertainty or fear change if I truly believed God sees every moment of my life and is already present in my future?

3. What area of my life do I need to place back into God's hands, trusting that the same God who guided Abraham, sustained Stephen, and stands watch over history is also watching over me right now?

Time For Prayer
Take a moment and communicate with God.

Cup 23
Acts 8:1-8

"So there was great joy in that city." vs. 8

Intense persecution broke out against the early church following the death of Stephen. Early believers fled into the neighboring cities and countries. As they went, they modeled the ministry of Jesus Christ. Their journeys were marked by their faithful sharing of the Gospel of Jesus Christ. The disciples were not silenced, even in the face of hatred. The haters wanted to silence the spread of the Gospel but their efforts only increased the spread of Jesus out into the world. The power of Jesus could not be silenced as many individuals heard the story of Jesus and experienced the healing power of salvation. In the place of intended silence, a wonderful ministry blossomed as Philip performed healings through the power of the Holy Spirit. A physical manifestation of healing took place and joy entered untold numbers of people. A ragged, persecuted people did not hate in return. They turned hatred into joy. Wherever they went, they left joy. Examine your life. What do you leave behind you? Can you say you leave joy behind? What actions can you take today to ensure people you interact with experience joy as you pass by?

Double Shot

1. When pressure or hostility rises in my own life, do I tend to pull back in silence, or do I allow the message and character of Jesus to keep shaping what I say and how I live?

2. How might God want to use the hard places I walk through to carry His healing and joy into the lives of others, just as He did with those early believers?

3. What intentional step can I take today so that the people I encounter are left with the joy of Christ rather than the weight of my circumstances or frustrations?

Time For Prayer
Take a moment and communicate with God.

"Give me this power also so that anyone I lay hands on may receive the Holy Spirit."
v. 19

Simon the "former" sorcerer should have taken a larger view of his life in Christ. He could only see what he might gain from Jesus, even after professing faith in Him. Even though Simon believed and was baptized, his actions demonstrated his faith was not yet grounded in true understanding. He did not stop to evaluate the new life he thought he had begun — a reminder of Peter's later encouragement to "grow in the grace and knowledge of our Lord" (2 Peter 3:18). Peter would not have had to say, "may your silver be destroyed with you". A life of discipleship is vital to moving forward spiritually. Simon made the mistake of not learning more about God before making an assumption. You can avoid a mistake like Simon by evaluating your spiritual life. Consider your life from a big picture perspective. Each step is part of a large story you are living. Ask God to develop a big picture view of your spiritual life as you make small steps to spiritual maturity.

Double Shot

1. Where might I be approaching Jesus with a narrow view, focusing on what I can gain rather than on growing deeper in understanding and discipleship?

2. What assumptions have I been making about my spiritual life that I need to bring before God so He can correct and reshape them?

3. How can I slow down today and ask God to help me see the bigger picture of my spiritual journey, rather than only the small steps right in front of me?

Time For Prayer
Take a moment and communicate with God.

Cup 25
Acts 8:26-40

"The Spirit told Philip, "Go and join that chariot." v.26

Philip did not know what was waiting for him on the road leading to Gaza. God had directed him to "go south to the road that goes down from Jerusalem". He obeyed God's command and headed out. Philip was privileged to share Jesus with a gentleman who was needing insight into Isaiah 53. Philip immediately began to explain the passage in light of Jesus. The eunuch placed his faith in Jesus and, filled with joy, commanded the chariot to stop so Philip could baptize him. What an encounter Philip had, all because he said yes to God in his life. We can experience God at work through us if we learn to simply say yes when He commands us to go out and work for the Kingdom. Have you learned to not only hear but obey the word of the Lord?

Double Shot

1. When God nudges me to take a step of obedience, even without knowing what awaits me, am I willing to simply say yes and trust Him with the outcome?

2. How open am I to the opportunities God places in front of me to share Jesus, even in ordinary or unexpected moments along the road?

3. What small act of obedience can I take today that might open the door for God to work through me in ways I cannot yet see?

Time For Prayer
Take a moment and communicate with God.

Cup 26
Acts 9:1-9

"Saul, Saul, why are you persecuting me?" v. 4

The salvation experience is different for each person, yet profoundly similar. Every disciple can easily identify with Saul, though experiences can be vastly different. He was persecuting Christians as seen in verse one. He was on a self-directed mission to stamp out the movement started by Jesus Christ. God had other plans for him. Before that bright encounter, he walked in spiritual darkness. When the glory of Jesus Christ and Saul collided, he fell to the ground. What drove him to the ground was the overwhelming presence of God. God personally visited him that day. The personal nature of the call of God is in the use of his name — Saul, Saul. Only a personal visit would break through his hardened heart to reveal the truth of his spiritual blindness. Have you heard Jesus call your name? Salvation is a personal encounter with God the Father through Jesus the Son. You may not have been struck down by the glory of God like Paul, but God knows your name and calls you to respond. Salvation is still available to those who are willing to hear Jesus call out to them. Have you heard your name called? If you have, did you respond in faith?

Double Shot

1. How clearly do I recognize the personal nature of God's call in my own life, and am I paying attention when He speaks my name through His Word and His Spirit?

2. In what ways might I still be walking in spiritual darkness or relying on my own direction instead of allowing the truth of Jesus to confront and reshape me?

3. If I have sensed Jesus calling me to respond in faith or obedience, how have I answered, and what step is He inviting me to take next?

Time For Prayer
Take a moment and communicate with God.

"Ananias went and entered the house. He placed his hands on him. . ." v. 17

Ministry involves Christians doing their part in the Kingdom. We discover through our spiritual gifts that God has a plan for believers. One notable willing minister is Ananias. He was an obedient, faithful, and discerning servant. God gave him an unexpected task, to go and tend to a new convert — Saul of Tarsus! He voiced a great concern to God about the assignment, but still obeyed. His role could be considered small when compared to others, yet his obedience was crucial in that moment. The early church would reap huge benefits from one humble servant obeying the voice of God. In 1 Corinthians 12:4-11, we learn that the Holy Spirit gives each believer a spiritual gift to be used for the Kingdom of God. The challenge is to discover and obediently use your gifts. Ananias' story takes only eight verses to tell, but the impact was felt for years to come. Do you know your spiritual gifts? Like Ananias, your obedience to God could shape lives and ripple into eternity. Never underestimate your obedience.

Double Shot

1. Am I willing to obey God even when the assignment feels unexpected, uncomfortable, or smaller than what I imagined my ministry to be?

2. How intentionally am I seeking to discover and use the spiritual gifts the Holy Spirit has given me for the good of the Kingdom?

3. What step of simple obedience can I take today, trusting that God can use even the smallest act to shape lives in ways I may never fully see?

Time For Prayer
Take a moment and communicate with God.

Cup 28
Acts 9:19b-31

"Saul was coming and going with them in Jerusalem, speaking boldly in the name of the Lord." v. 28

Saul's life changed in a moment. One moment, a life dedicated to the destruction of the early church was radically transformed by an encounter with the risen Jesus Christ of Nazareth. The experience on the road to Damascus brought an observable change in Saul. He grew in his faith and proved through Scripture that Jesus was the Messiah. Death threats did not stop him from declaring what he had come to know as the absolute truth of the Gospel. Saul's encounter with Jesus became a deep-seated conviction, a truth he would later express in Romans 1:16. Saul's boldness came from the empowering of the Holy Spirit. Does your passion for Jesus reflect the same boldness Saul showed? Consider the difference Jesus has made in your life. Do you wish others to have the same experience and salvation? Does it drive you to do your best to overcome obstacles when it comes to sharing the Good News? Ask God to help you have passion and boldness for Him.

Double Shot

1. In what areas of my life do I see the most noticeable transformation because of my encounter with Jesus, and how can I more boldly share that change with others?

2. When faced with obstacles or fear, what can I do to tap into the Holy Spirit's power and find the boldness to share the Gospel, just like Saul did?

3. Do I truly desire others to experience the same life-changing encounter with Jesus that I have had? How can I align my actions, conversations, and prayers to reflect that passion?

Time For Prayer
Take a moment and communicate with God.

Cup 29
Acts 9:32-43

"This became known throughout Joppa, and many believed in the Lord." v. 42

Everywhere Jesus went, He ministered to those in need. Peter adopted that style as well. His travels gave him the opportunity to heal a paralyzed man and then raise Dorcas from the dead. His actions were not planned out, ministry naturally occurred. People in need were not overlooked or viewed as insignificant. They were viewed as individuals who needed a touch from God. Peter was willing to reach out and not only share the Gospel, but also demonstrate the power of the Holy Spirit through a healing touch. The wonderful result of the miracles was many turned and experienced the ultimate healing, salvation. Your efforts at ministry can follow Jesus and Peter's model. Ministry does not have to be difficult when you view your life as a journey with opportunities to reach others with the message of Jesus. Pray as Peter prayed and allow the Holy Spirit to shape your view of ministry. Where in your life could you minister in a natural way? Where do your opportunities arise — caring for a neighbor, listening to a co-worker, praying for someone?

Double Shot

1. How can I begin to see everyday moments as opportunities for ministry by being more aware of the people around me who might need a touch from God?

2. What natural talents or resources do I have that I could use to meet the needs of others and share the love of Jesus in a practical way?

3. Are there specific relationships or situations in my life where I feel God is calling me to step in with a healing touch, whether that's through prayer, a kind word, or simply being present? How can I take action today?

Time For Prayer
Take a moment and communicate with God.

Cup 30
Acts 10:1-7

"He was a devout man and feared God along with his whole household." v. 2

You encounter a new character in the Book of Acts, a centurion named Cornelius. He is described in verses one and two as devoted to God. He had a deep desire to know more and have a real relationship, not just a passing familiarity. God heard his prayers and responded. God honored Cornelius's openness, and in His grace revealed Himself — not as a reward for his passion, but in response to a heart open to Him. Cornelius received his heart's desire. This was a huge moment for him. His story reminds us that God's salvation plan is for all people. Everyone who opens their heart to Him can be saved. Do you have an all-consuming passion to know more of God? Is your heart set on a deep relationship not settling for a passing familiarity? Who you are as a person is laid bare before our Creator through your passions. Scary? Yes! Necessary? Absolutely! You can have monumental movements with God as well when you spend time in prayer seeking God's face. Evaluate what you desire and take that desire to God. Seek God and you will discover He responds!

Double Shot

1. Am I truly passionate about knowing God more deeply, or have I settled for just a surface-level familiarity with Him? How can I cultivate a deeper relationship with God?

2. In what areas of my life do I need to be more open and vulnerable before God, allowing Him to reveal more of Himself to me?

3. How can I make time for regular, intentional prayer to seek God's face and invite Him into the deeper desires of my heart, trusting that He will respond?

Time For Prayer
Take a moment and communicate with God.

Cup 31
Acts 10:8-16

"I have never eaten anything impure and ritually unclean." v. 14

Peter knew the Jewish rules and regulations of what was clean and unclean. When God requested of him to eat what was forbidden, he was confronted by his past and it became a temporary roadblock to obedience. Peter learned a lesson that eventful day. Never let your past determine your present obedience. Peter was the sum of his experiences, but those experiences prevented him from learning in the moment. God sought to prepare Peter for the tremendous task of preaching to Cornelius. The command was simple but struck at the core God desired to change. Peter would have missed out on a great lesson that day if he would have allowed his past to override his current command to be obedient. May we be like Peter. Acknowledge your past but do not let it hinder your obedience today. Your past experiences, though they have molded who we are, can become roadblocks to what God is trying to teach you today. Your past has shaped who you are, but it should never shape your obedience more than God's present voice. Ask Him for discernment so your history becomes a tool for wisdom, not a barrier to growth.

Double Shot

1. How does my past, whether good or bad, affect the way I respond to God's commands today? Are there areas where I've allowed past experiences to shape or limit my obedience?

2. In what areas of my life is God calling me to step out in obedience, even if it challenges my previous understanding or comfort zones?

3. What lessons from my past can I use as wisdom for growth, but not as barriers to my current obedience?

Time For Prayer
Take a moment and communicate with God.

Cup 32
Acts 10:17-23

"Get up, go downstairs, and go with them with no doubts at all because I have sent them." v. 20

Peter did not have long to ponder the message of the vision before he was instructed to greet and travel with Cornelius' servants. In an instant, Peter was confronted with the issue of Jew and Gentile, clean versus unclean. We know Peter was starting to get God's message when he invited the Gentile servants to stay and lodge with him. Some lessons need to steep in your heart, but they always find ways to be used in our lives at one point or another. This lesson would find a greater application when God prompted the early disciples to accept Gentiles into the early church as fellow disciples of Jesus(Acts 11:1-18). God is practical, even the lessons that confuse us at first are training for the mission He is preparing us to fulfill. You may be tempted to say, "I cannot change!" or "This is the way I was raised!" Those are excuses you use to prevent spiritual growth, but you can determine to allow God to shape you. Be available and open to His lessons — You never know when God will call you to use what He has been teaching you.

Double Shot

1. What areas in my life am I holding onto old beliefs or patterns that God is calling me to reconsider, even though they may seem uncomfortable or unfamiliar?

2. When was the last time I took a step of faith to welcome someone or something that seemed "unclean" or outside my comfort zone?

3. How can I stay open to God's lessons, even when they don't make sense at first, trusting that He is preparing me for something greater?

Time For Prayer
Take a moment and communicate with God.

Cup 33
Acts 10:24-33

"Send someone to Joppa and invite Simon here." vs 32

God is always at work in our lives. He leads and guides us in order to grow us into the men and women we are to be in Christ. The lessons He imparts prepare us to be used in tremendous ways if we are teachable. Of course, we do not know precisely when the lessons we learn will be used as we work in the Kingdom. We are simply called to be open and moldable; God does the rest. The results of life lessons may not appear to be of any value at the moment, but a moment does come when we look back at the movements of God. It is as if God builds a beautiful watch, with gears, cogs, and springs working in perfect unison to bring the watch to life. We marvel at the watch as a whole, but it could never work if the individual pieces resisted being molded and formed as they were put into place. Peter and Cornelius were unaware of one another at the beginning, but God had prepared both men for this moment in time fitting their stories together like pieces in His divine design. Just as every part of a watch has purpose, so every season of growth matters. May we learn to be humble and open before Jesus. Let's embrace the lessons that are meant for our good and the growth of the Kingdom.

Double Shot

1. Am I willing to trust that even the seasons of life that seem mundane or painful are part of God's perfect design?

2. In what areas of my life might I be resisting God's molding?

3. How can I become more aware of God's hand at work in my life day-to-day, even in the smallest moments?

Time For Prayer
Take a moment and communicate with God.

Cup 34
Acts 10:34-48

"We ourselves are witnesses of everything He did." vs 39

"All for Christ!" The phrase is a great way to sum up one's purpose in living life. All that we are and do should be to the glory of Jesus Christ of Nazareth. Nothing is left out. Our entire lives, inside and out, should come under this phrase. Peter, when given the opportunity, shared the Good News. It is Jesus who transforms. Nothing in this life changes us like knowing Him. Peter knew it and he shared that message with Cornelius and his family. We are to do the same. When given a chance, we are to share Jesus. No one changes a person like Jesus can. When a person accepts the message about Jesus, all of creation convulses and applauds as a person receives new life through the Holy Spirit. Another person praising and worshiping God. Another person declaring the greatness of Jesus. Another person bearing witness to the transforming power of Jesus. May "All for Christ" not just be a phrase we say, but a life we live so that the world may see and know the transforming power of Jesus.

Double Shot

1. Reflect on how you live out your faith in your everyday actions, decisions, and interactions. What are some practical steps you can take to ensure that everything you do points back to Christ and brings glory to Him?

2. When was the last time I shared the Good News with someone?

3. Take time to reflect on areas where you may be holding back from fully surrendering to Christ. Is there a part of your heart, mind, or behavior that still needs His touch? How can you invite Him into that space to bring about change and renewal?

Time For Prayer
Take a moment and communicate with God.

Cup 35
Acts 11:1-18

"Peter began to explain to them step by step." v. 4

Testimony is a vital part of a believer's life. Peter was called upon to explain how God accepted the Gentiles into His Kingdom. Peter does not go into a lengthy theological lecture. Instead, he relates his story. He used no theological terms to explain what happened; Peter simply testified how God prepared him for the arrival of Cornelius' messengers. He shared how he witnessed God pouring out the Holy Spirit on both Jewish and Gentile men and women. The result was that the Jewish believers glorified God, and the bond between Jew and Gentile grew stronger. Your testimony is important, for it reveals the movement and revelation of God in you. Just like Peter, you do not have to take people to theology school. Simply recall a moment when God moved in your life and share it with someone who needs hope. His impact upon your life is a testimony to others of the saving grace they too can experience, and it brings glory to God.

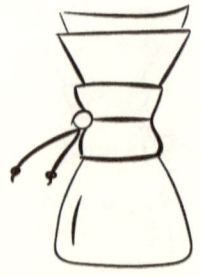

Double Shot

1. Reflect on whether you've been holding back from sharing your story because you think it needs to sound polished or theological. How can you return to the simplicity of just telling someone what God has done in your life?

2. What recent moment in my walk with God could be a source of hope for someone else? Who in your life might need to hear your story?

3. How might God use my testimony to strengthen someone's faith or even heal a division?

Time For Prayer
Take a moment and communicate with God.

Cup 36
Acts 11:19-26

"And large numbers of people were added to the Lord." v. 24

The early church grew rapidly, and with growth came the great need for discipleship. Seeing the seriousness of the need, Barnabas recognized he could not fulfill all of the demands alone. What did he do? He sought out a man he knew could help. The one chosen by Barnabas to join forces with was Saul, and together they made tremendous progress. One word describes what Barnabas demonstrated, synergy. Synergy means we accomplish more together than we ever could alone. Work in God's Kingdom can be a lot of fun when we recognize we need one another. We are not to minister alone in the Kingdom. When others come alongside us in the work, the results can astound us. We may not be the one asking, rather, we may be the one being asked to help. Do not be hasty to say no, rush to say yes! Help carry the burden of ministry alongside others and observe just how much can be done by the group. Look around and find a way to experience the joy of synergy, living out Ecclesiastes 4:9 in your own life.

Double Shot

1. Where am I trying to carry the work of God's Kingdom alone when He never asked me to?

2. Am I willing to say "yes" when someone asks me to join them in ministry?

3. Who around me could I encourage, invite, or partner with so that we can accomplish more together than we could ever do alone?

Time For Prayer
Take a moment and communicate with God.

Cup 37
Acts 12:1-19

"but the church was praying fervently to God for him." v.5

One lesson we learn from the early church is how to handle times of persecution. Being a believer requires stamina and perseverance. We must not take our connection to Jesus lightly. Jesus told us in Matthew 10:22 about the persecution that will come our way because we are His followers. Peter found himself in prison awaiting execution for being a follower of Jesus. Once the early church heard of the situation, they did exactly what was needed: they came together, united in prayer. In response to their prayers, God delivered him from prison. Like Peter, you may face a situation that seems hopeless, but prayer is still your most powerful response. God may not deliver you as Peter, but He will answer and provide exactly what you need to endure. When difficult situations come, don't wait, pray now for the strength to stay faithful. Pray for strength to endure to the end, even if the path leads to death.

Double Shot

1. Consider how quickly you move toward God when trouble comes. What would it look like for prayer to become your first response rather than your last resort?

2. Consider the situations that weigh heavily on your heart. Who could stand with you in united prayer so that you do not carry the burden alone?

3. How can I grow in endurance so that I remain faithful even when God's answer is different from what I hoped for?

Time For Prayer
Take a moment and communicate with God.

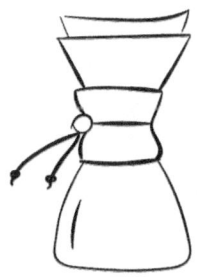

Cup 38
Acts 12:20-25

"But the word of God flourished and multiplied." v. 24

When persecution arises, we can be assured God's will and plan will never be stopped. God takes care of His people, His enemies, and His Kingdom. Our hope in the midst of difficulty is found in the finished, accomplished work of Jesus on Calvary. Whether we live or die, our future is secure. The enemies of God will experience judgment instead of hope. Herod arrogantly attempted to take God's place. It was a futile attempt to replace the sovereign God of the universe. As a result of God's providence, His Kingdom will flourish. Man can never and will never be able to thwart God's purpose for creation. We can live with assurance and hope that while we may experience persecution for a season, God will prevail and His Kingdom will flourish and grow so others may have the opportunity to be saved. Where is your hope? What is the foundation of your hope for the future? Evaluate your life and if you have not placed your faith in Jesus, consider doing so now. Jesus died on a cross to pay the penalty for your sins so you may have genuine hope for the future.

Double Shot

1. Am I truly resting in the unshakeable hope Jesus secured for me on Calvary, or am I allowing present pressures and persecution to dictate my peace?

2. Where in my life am I tempted to take control instead of surrendering to the sovereign God whose plans can never be stopped?

3. If God's Kingdom will prevail and flourish no matter what, how should that truth reshape the way I face hardship, respond to opposition, and steward every opportunity for others to hear about Jesus?

Time For Prayer
Take a moment and communicate with God.

Cup 39
Acts 13:1-3

"Set apart for me Barnabas and Saul for the work to which I have called them." v.2

Our life as believers is not one of isolation. The verses under consideration demonstrate the importance of Kingdom life and participation. God could have called each of the men mentioned individually, but He chose to accomplish His work in a corporate setting. First, the men were worshiping the Lord with the church. As they worshiped, their hearts were open to the Holy Spirit's leading. Second, they received instruction from God as they were in worship. In corporate worship, we are encouraged by others' openness before God, which helps us open our own hearts. Finally, the church not only confirmed their call but also supported their ministry. Receiving encouragement from other believers is invaluable as we seek to obey God. We are called to live and minister alongside others. Get involved in a local church and allow God to use you. If you are not part of a church, ask God to guide you to one and join in the work. May God remind you that you are never alone in His work, but part of His body, the Church.

Double Shot

1. Am I intentionally placing myself in environments of corporate worship where my heart can stay open to the Holy Spirit's leading, or have I drifted toward an isolated, "on-my-own" version of the Christian life?

2. How willing am I to receive encouragement, confirmation, or even correction from the body of Christ so that my calling and obedience can be strengthened rather than stalled?

3. If God designed me to live and minister alongside others, what practical step do I need to take to engage more faithfully in a local church and allow God to use me for His Kingdom purposes?

Time For Prayer
Take a moment and communicate with God.

Cup 40
Acts 13:4-12

"Arriving in Salamis, they proclaimed the word of God." v. 5

Barnabas and Saul (Paul) set out on their first journey after being set apart by the church in Antioch. Landing at Salamis, they began the work of sharing the message of Jesus. As they traveled across the island, they encountered a wide variety of people. They would learn to depend upon the empowering of the Holy Spirit to handle each one. The Holy Spirit was key to helping them reach each person they encountered such as Bar-Jesus, Sergius Paulus, and Elymas. Each one required a different approach, and Paul relied on God for the wisdom to reach them. Just as Paul and Barnabas faced different responses to the Gospel, you too meet many kinds of people and challenges each day. Do you allow the Holy Spirit to guide your words and actions like Paul and Barnabas? Your courage to share can rise to the challenges you encounter when you recognize God wishes to give you what you need in the moment. Where do you need the Spirit's guidance most? At home? At work? With friends? Wherever you are, the same Spirit who guided Paul and Barnabas is ready to guide you today.

Double Shot

1. As I move through my day and encounter all kinds of people, am I truly depending on the Holy Spirit's guidance, or am I relying on my own instincts and experience to navigate conversations?

2. Where do I most need the Spirit's wisdom right now, at home, at work, with friends, or in some situation I've been avoiding?

3. When challenges arise or responses to the Gospel differ, am I willing to slow down long enough to ask, "Holy Spirit, what should I do or say in this moment?"

Time For Prayer
Take a moment and communicate with God.

Cup 41
Acts 13:13-52

"Fellow Israelites, and you who fear God, Listen!" v 16

The Gospel story is a wonderful story that never grows old. God has been and is wonderfully active in the world He created. He does not wish for us to be wayward and to die in our sinfulness. Our lives are to be given over to this story. The Gospel is not to be kept on a shelf in our homes, on a coffee table in our living rooms, or tucked away in the recesses of our hearts. We are to take the Gospel into the world and proclaim it clearly and boldly. We do not have to be scholars or have every verse of Scripture memorized. All we are commanded to do is simply tell all we meet the story of God the Father. As Paul declared in Acts 13:38, 'Through this man forgiveness of sins is being proclaimed to you.' The same message is ours to share. Note that Paul and Barnabas did not launch into a detailed exegesis of some miniscule theological point. They simply shared the Gospel story of God and His salvation story for humanity. The result was many believed in Jesus and came to faith. The same opportunity stands before us today. Can you tell a story? Next time you are engaged in conversation, share Jesus' story.

Double Shot

1. Have I grown silent or hesitant with the Gospel, keeping it tucked away rather than taking the simple, bold step of telling others the story of Jesus?

2. Do I over complicate evangelism, forgetting that God only asks me to share the story—not to be a scholar, debate expert, or theological encyclopedia?

3. Who in my life needs to hear the story of God's forgiveness, and am I willing to step into my next conversation ready to share Jesus naturally and clearly?

Time For Prayer
Take a moment and communicate with God.

Cup 42
Acts 14:1-20

"So they stayed there a long time and spoke boldly for the Lord."

v. 3

Two groups clearly emerge from those with whom we share the Gospel. One group is interested and may surrender their lives to Jesus as Lord and Savior. A second group takes offense at the Gospel. They do not wish to hear about sin, judgment, or salvation. Their hearts are hardened, which can lead them to oppose or persecute the messenger. Paul and Barnabas experienced both responses in Iconium and Lystra. Yet through it all, they relied upon the Holy Spirit for strength to endure both praise and persecution. Had they not been prepared, the praise of the people could have become an avenue for pride, robbing God of His glory. How do you handle praise? Praise can be one of the hardest tests to overcome because we naturally enjoy the approval of others. Persecution, though painful, is easier to understand because we do not want to be disliked. So, how do we remain balanced and focused? We can begin by recognizing our weaknesses to both responses. Then ask God to make us spiritually strong. Pray that He will help you stay humble when praised and steadfast when opposed—so that in all things, His glory alone will shine through your life.

Double Shot

1. How do I respond when people speak well of me—do I quietly absorb the praise, or do I consciously direct the glory back to God?

2. When opposition or rejection comes because of my faith, do I retreat in fear, or do I ask the Holy Spirit for strength to remain steady and steadfast?

3. In which area of my life do I most need God to make me spiritually strong, even when praised or opposed?

Time For Prayer
Take a moment and communicate with God.

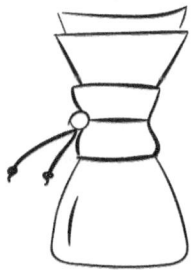

Cup 43
Acts 14:21-28

"strengthening the disciples by encouraging them to continue in the faith" v. 22

The work of Christ is comprehensive; it reaches hearts, transforms lives, and calls believers to both share and disciple. Everywhere Paul journeyed, he sowed seeds of the Gospel. The Book of Acts recounts Paul's missionary endeavors in detail, but it also highlights Paul's dedication to discipleship. He shared the mindset of Jesus in Matthew 9:37. Paul longed not only to spread the Gospel, but also to see those who accepted Jesus grow in their faith. Verses 22 and 23 reveal that Paul also invested in believers so that spiritual growth could occur. He shared Jesus with any who would listen, and he encouraged growth. Ministry must remain balanced between evangelism and discipleship. We are to not only share the Gospel, but also to disciple those who come to know Christ through our efforts. No wonder Jesus stated that workers were needed for the Kingdom. Maintaining a balanced ministry is challenging, but possible when we allow God to work through us. Do you share your faith? Do you disciple those who are new in the faith?

Double Shot

1. In what ways do you actively seek to balance both evangelism and discipleship in your life?

2. Reflect on your attitude toward sharing your faith. Are you motivated by a genuine desire to see others come to Christ and grow in their walk with Him?

3. What challenges do you face in making evangelism and discipleship part of your regular routine?

Time For Prayer
Take a moment and communicate with God.

Cup 44
Acts 15:1-5

"After Paul and Barnabas had engaged them in serious argument and debate." v. 2

Believers constantly face challenges to their faith. When Paul faced the challenge of false teaching being introduced into the Gospel, he was courageous and confronted it head-on. He was unwilling to allow others to corrupt and pervert the truth of Jesus Christ. He and Barnabas "engaged them in serious argument and debate". Paul recognized the importance of preserving the purity of the Gospel message. Salvation is vital to all of us. Changing the tiniest part of the truth of the Gospel has eternal consequences. Salvation is by faith in Jesus Christ alone, and when that is changed, we lose truth. When one truth is compromised, others soon follow, and eventually the message of salvation itself is lost. Can you spot challenges to your faith? Do you feel prepared to meet those challenges? You can stand for the truth with a well-prepared defense. We are not called to be ugly toward those who distort the Gospel, but we must be courageous and take a stand. We can prepare ourselves by studying Scripture and learning how to explain it with love and clarity.

Double Shot

1. What false teachings or distortions of the Gospel have you encountered? How did you respond? What could you do differently next time to stand firm in the truth?

2. What steps can you take to strengthen your understanding and ability to stand firm in the face of opposition?

3. In what ways can you engage with others who distort the Gospel without compromising your witness?

Time For Prayer
Take a moment and communicate with God.

Cup 45
Acts 15:6-35

"The whole assembly became silent and listened." v. 12

We can feel alone when we stand for the truth of the Gospel. When we are willing to take a stand, there can be a tremendous overflow of courage from our heart to the hearts of others. They may wish to make a stand for the truth as well, but it often takes the courage and example of another to stir them to action. Peter gives a report to the early church in Jerusalem about the salvation of Cornelius, who was a Gentile. Paul and Barnabas then stood and testified about their witness to the work of the Holy Spirit among the Gentiles. The early church responded by sending a letter of clarification to the church in Antioch. The strength of Peter, Paul, and Barnabas had a positive effect upon the early church. Your courage to stand for truth can impact others around you. Be steadfast in your faith, for you never know who may need to see courageous faith. Your example as a disciple boldly standing up for the truth of Jesus Christ in the power of the Spirit can inspire others. May your Spirit-led boldness reflect the faithfulness of the apostles and encourage others to stand firm in the truth of Jesus Christ.

Double Shot

1. How has someone else's example of courage in standing for truth impacted your faith?

2. Think about your own interactions with fellow believers. How can your example of steadfastness inspire others to take a bold stand for the Gospel? What steps can you take today to encourage others to be firm in their faith?

3. Are there any areas in your life where you have been hesitant to stand for truth?

Time For Prayer
Take a moment and communicate with God.

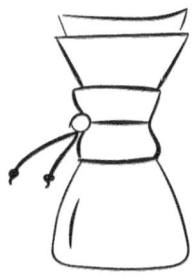

Cup 46
Acts 15:36-41

"They had such a sharp disagreement that they parted company."
v. 39

Paul and Barnabas had a dispute, in fact, a personal disagreement. How these men handled their differences stands as a testimony to the work of God in their lives. They desired to be the most effective for God, but they had differences of opinion when it came to John Mark. Their disagreement was emotionally tense, not superficial, since their dispute led to a parting of ways. What seemed like a setback became a new opportunity. God used their parting for His purposes; two ministering parties sprang to life from the one. Paul would lead one and Barnabas would lead another. Eventually, Paul reconciled with John Mark. From their experience, we learn to wish one another well even in the midst of conflict. We do not have to agree all the time. If you disagree with someone, do not tear one another down, but allow God to turn your conflict into an opportunity for greater service.

Double Shot

1. When you face a disagreement with another believer, are you more focused on winning the argument or allowing God to shape your heart through it?

2. Is there someone in your life you need to release with grace even if you don't see eye to eye?

3. How might God want to turn a present conflict in your life into an opportunity for greater ministry or spiritual growth?

Time For Prayer
Take a moment and communicate with God.

Cup 47
Acts 16:1-5

"Paul wanted Timothy to go with him." v. 3

Our last devotion brought to our attention the creation of two missionary groups in the place of one. Paul headed out and it was not long before he discovered great potential in a young man by the name of Timothy. Recognizing Timothy's abilities, Paul invited him into ministry, beginning a lifelong partnership. Mentorship is not just the ability to pass on skills and knowledge, but the willingness to invest in the life of another. Timothy would become one of the early church's pastors and a lifelong friend of Paul. They ministered side by side and witnessed the churches grow as they engaged in discipleship. Just as Paul saw potential in Timothy, do you look at others as a potential ministry partner? As a believer in Jesus, we are not to sit on the sidelines, but to intentionally invest in someone God has placed in our lives. Pray for God's wisdom to see the person you are called to invest in.

Double Shot

1. Who in your life shows signs of spiritual potential, and are you willing to take a step toward investing in them intentionally?

2. Are you asking God regularly to open your eyes to the person He wants you to mentor or encourage in the faith?

3. In what ways can you move from the sidelines of ministry to active engagement in someone else's spiritual development this week?

Time For Prayer
Take a moment and communicate with God.

Cup 48
Acts 16:6-15

"The Spirit of Jesus did not allow them" v. 7

Life with God involves both knowing and doing His will. Paul modeled this balance as he listened to the Spirit's guidance and acted in obedience. Paul was focused not only on sound theology but also on obedience to God's direction. He was concerned about knowing where God was guiding his life. Because he desired to serve effectively, Paul was attentive to the Holy Spirit's direction. Paul responded to the Holy Spirit and set out for Macedonia. Many wonderful people benefitted from his ministry. Paul's obedience opened the door for God's work in Macedonia. Because he followed the Spirit's prompting, Lydia and her household came to faith. All this began with one man's willingness to follow the Holy Spirit's direction. When was the last time you felt the Spirit's prompting? Did you follow it? We need to ask the hard questions that focus us on our willingness to obey God's commands. When we are obedient to God, He can accomplish great things through us.

Double Shot

1. When was the last time you sensed the Spirit nudging you, and did you take the step He placed before you?

2. What keeps you from acting on God's prompting? How will you surrender that to Him today?

3. If God opened a "Macedonia-sized" opportunity in your life, would He find you attentive and willing to obey?

Time For Prayer
Take a moment and communicate with God.

Cup 49
Acts 16:16-40

"About midnight Paul and Silas were singing hymns to God."
v. 25

This is one of those childhood Bible stories that continues to inspire us. A theme that runs through this story is deliverance. As Jesus came to deliver, Paul and Silas, through the power of the Holy Spirit, deliver a slave woman from the oppression of Satan. Her owners, angered at their loss of profit, dragged Paul and Silas before the city officials, where they were beaten and jailed. Not to be discouraged, as Paul and Silas were praying and singing hymns to God, and the prisoners were listening to them. God miraculously delivers them in the middle of the night. The soldier, fearing the worst, planned to take his own life, but Paul called out and as a result, the soldier and his household were delivered from their sin upon hearing of the Gospel. God is a God of deliverance. Regardless of where we may find ourselves in the story, we can expect God to deliver. One word of caution must be noted. When God delivers, that deliverance may be the deliverance we desire as in the case of salvation. It may also come in a way that we cannot fathom on this side of eternity. Today, wherever you feel bound, God's deliverance is sure, even if it comes in ways beyond our understanding.

Double Shot

1. Where in your life do you feel bound or pressed in, and have you trusted God to deliver, even if His deliverance looks different than you expected?

2. How can you imitate Paul and Silas by worshiping and praying even in the middle of your "midnight hour"?

3. Who around you needs to hear the message of deliverance, and will you be attentive to those divine moments God may place in your path?

Time For Prayer
Take a moment and communicate with God.

Cup 50
Acts 17:1-9

"These men who have turned the world upside down have come here too." v. 6

Paul and Silas had a plan to follow. Each town they entered was treated in the same way. Luke used the phrase, "as usual" to describe the way they approached sharing the Gospel of Jesus Christ. Paul began by sharing in the synagogue, giving his audience time to respond. They were intentional in their approach, following a consistent plan wherever they went. Though each town was different, Paul shared the same message. Paul followed God's plan through presenting Jesus and proving that it was necessary for Him to suffer and rise from the dead. As a result, a large number of people came to know Jesus. Not everyone was happy with Paul and Silas, yet their message changed lives. Can others observe your message as a transforming message? Just as Paul and Silas were intentional about sharing Christ, you too can plan to share wherever you go. Place a Gospel tract or engage in spiritual conversation. Ask God to open your eyes to divine appointments He gives you to share.

Double Shot

1. Is there an "as usual" pattern in your life that consistently points others to Jesus, or is that something God is calling you to establish?

2. Who might God place in your path today if you simply walked with intentionality and spiritual readiness?

3. List a few practical steps can you take to make sharing Christ a natural part of your daily rhythm?

Time For Prayer
Take a moment and communicate with God.

Cup 51
Acts 17:10-21

"So he reasoned in the synagogue with the Jews" v. 17

Though Paul faced difficult circumstances, he kept on sharing his faith with whoever would engage in conversation. Even when Paul fled for his life, he arrived in Athens with the same willingness to try again. Paul refused to let yesterday's trials define today's opportunities. The people of Athens were open to hearing about Jesus. While some did not want to hear, some were willing to dialogue with Paul about Jesus. If Paul allowed the pains of yesterday to affect his present, then the people of Athens would have missed an opportunity to hear the message of the Gospel. Paul would have missed an opportunity to fulfill his calling to share. He met the people where they were, in the synagogue, marketplace, and at home, showing that the message of Jesus could be shared in every part of life. Do you continue sharing Jesus even when experiencing rejection? You can be just as committed as Paul. Do not let your yesterday be a hindrance to your sharing today. Ask God to help you rise above the discouragements of the past and empower you to share boldly in the present.

Double Shot

1. Where am I letting old wounds or past rejection talk me out of sharing Jesus today, and what would it look like to step forward anyway?

2. Who in my daily routine might be more spiritually open than I assume, if I were actually willing to engage?

3. What specific discouragement from yesterday do I need to place before God so I can share boldly in the present?

Time For Prayer
Take a moment and communicate with God.

Cup 52
Acts 17:22-34

"Therefore, what you worship in ignorance, this I proclaim to you"
v. 23b

Paul had only been in Athens a short time. After trouble in Thessalonica forced him to leave, he arrived in Athens seeking a safe haven. As he walked and observed the city, his heart became concerned. Athens was a great center of learning filled with philosophers who loved to pursue wisdom. When he saw the altar dedicated to the 'unknown God', his compassion deepened. He wanted them to realize that the true God is not distant but near, waiting to be found by those who seek Him. Paul shared the Gospel, the story of the resurrected Christ, giving them the opportunity to repent and place their faith in Jesus Christ. Like Paul, you are called to share the Good News with others in your life. Be creative and use your everyday experiences, habits, and hobbies to guide conversations toward Jesus. Take a fresh look at your daily activities and notice the opportunities God gives you to share Jesus with those you encounter. Ask God to open your heart to His divine opportunities today.

Double Shot

1. What everyday routines or hobbies could I use as natural bridges to talk about Jesus instead of waiting for the perfect moment?

2. Where have I grown dull to the spiritual need around me, and what would it take for my compassion to stay awake?

3. How can I invite God to help me notice the "unknown gods" in the lives of people I know so I can point them to the One who is near?

Time For Prayer
Take a moment and communicate with God.

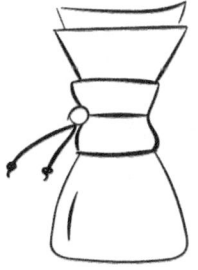

Cup 53
Acts 18:1-17

The Lord said to Paul in a night vision, "Don't be afraid, but keep on speaking and don't be silent." vs 9

All believers will face rejection, whether from family, friends or co-workers, for their faith in Jesus Christ. Even Paul faced opposition as he traveled. Now in Corinth, he faces opposition again in the synagogue due to his message about Jesus. Paul remained faithful and was used to establish a solid church in Corinth. He met and ministered alongside Aquila and Priscilla. Together they encouraged each other. You can find similar strength as Paul. Jesus has given you His promise and presence. (Matthew 28:20) You are not alone. You can stand firm even if the opposition comes from a family member or even a spouse. Standing firm testifies of the grace of God. Seek out other believers and partner together to strengthen one another. Work together as Paul did with his companions. Ask God to develop a keen discernment of His presence within. Consider a situation where you may encounter misunderstanding or rejection for your faith. How could you respond that would provide a testimony for Jesus and His grace and mercy?

Double Shot

1. What situation in my life right now requires me to stand firm in my faith even if it risks misunderstanding or rejection?

2. Who has God placed around me to encourage and strengthen my faith, and how can I partner with them more intentionally?

3. How could my response to opposition become a living testimony of Jesus' grace and steadiness?

Time For Prayer
Take a moment and communicate with God.

Cup 54
Acts 18:18-23

"After spending some time there, he set out, traveling through one place after another in the region of Galatia and Phrygia, strengthening all the disciples." vs 23

Our investment in others is a lifelong endeavor. We do not speak one word, perform one action, or encourage one time. Investing in the lives of other disciples in God's Kingdom requires perseverance. As investing in the stock market is a long term process to see results, so our spiritual impact in others is similar. The process of mentoring is repeated throughout our lives. We teach, encourage, and even correct over and over again. God takes our perseverance in ministry and reaps a harvest in their lives. In our culture of hurry, this type of investment seems counter productive. We demand instant results and when those results do not appear, we move on to something else more promising. Let us learn a lesson from Paul in this verse. Take time to visit! Spend time with the ones God has placed in your life and allow the Holy Spirit to guide you. Ask God for guidance and strength to invest in the ones in your life He has given to you.

Double Shot

1. Who has God placed in my life that needs long term spiritual investment, not a one time boost?

2. Where am I expecting instant results in someone's spiritual growth instead of trusting God to work over time?

3. How can I slow down this week and be physically present with the people God has entrusted to me?

Time For Prayer
Take a moment and communicate with God.

Cup 55
Acts 18:24-28

"For he vigorously refuted the Jews in Public, demonstrating through the Scriptures that Jesus is the Messiah." vs 28

You are introduced to a gentleman by the name of Apollos in this section. He represents the competence you should strive to attain. You are not to study Scripture to have a general knowledge of facts and ideas. Your knowledge should lead you to have the ability to defend the Gospel and to demonstrate Jesus of Nazareth is the Messiah, God's Christ(anointed one). You want your doctor to have a deeper understanding of the body beyond what he could learn from the internet. A deeper understanding of human anatomy is expected. Many believers know the general flow of the Bible. Knowing the basic Bible stories is elementary knowledge. What is needed today is the knowledge of how the Scriptures point to and prove Jesus of Nazareth is God incarnate. Take that important understanding and share it with others around you. They need to know Jesus has secured salvation for all of humanity. Push yourself beyond the mere elementary things of the Bible. Dive deep and allow the Holy Spirt to make connections for you and equip you to share Jesus with others.

Double Shot

1. Where do I need to move beyond basic familiarity with Scripture and pursue a deeper understanding that strengthens my ability to share Jesus?

2. What specific step(s) can I take this week to grow in confidence when explaining who Jesus is and why it matters?

3. Who in my life needs to hear the deeper truths of Scripture, not just the familiar stories?

Time For Prayer
Take a moment and communicate with God.

Cup 56
Acts 19:1-10

"When they heard this, they were baptized into the name of the Lord Jesus." vs 5

One challenge we face as a disciple of Jesus is depth of spiritual development. As His disciple, we are called to study and learn as much as we can. Knowing the ways and workings of God places us in the position to not only know but to do what pleases Him. A firm foundation forms within us as we grow. Paul encountered a group of individuals who were on the same journey as he was but not as far along. Their willingness to learn more about God and His provision of the Messiah(Jesus Christ of Nazareth), opened a door of acceptance within their hearts. Their reception of the Gospel resulted in their salvation through the Holy Spirit. As a result of their salvation, the Spirit was able to form deep foundational roots. These foundational roots are similar to a large tree's root which grows deep into the ground. These deep roots stabilize the tree when strong winds and storms come its way. The Holy Spirit can form the same foundation in us when we seek to grow in Christ. Stimulate your spiritual growth and study God's Word, spend time in prayer, and apply God's principles. Let the storms come, you will be firm in Jesus!

Double Shot

1. What habits in my life are actually helping my spiritual roots grow deeper, and which ones are holding me back?

2. Where am I sensing the Holy Spirit nudging me to learn more so I can mature in my faith?

3. How can I build stronger foundations through Scripture, prayer, and obedience before the next storm shows up?

Time For Prayer
Take a moment and communicate with God.

Cup 57
Acts 19:11-20

The evil spirit answered them, "I know Jesus, and I recognize Paul—but who are you?" vs 15

You cannot fake a relationship with Jesus Christ. The sons of Sceva learned this the hard way. Paul was working and proclaiming Jesus through message and actions (Holy Spirit through Paul). The men misunderstood and thought they could appropriate the name of Jesus without having a genuine relationship. They were wrong and paid a high price for their lack of integrity. Their mistake notes a deeper truth; God moves in remarkable ways when you are genuinely connected to Him. What you do is grounded in a faith relationship. The Holy Spirit within guides you to minister where He directs. You move at His command and He is responsible for the results. When your relationship is paired with the empowering of the Holy Spirit, He does the impossible through you. Others who heard of the event were drawn to Jesus. They demonstrated they were devoted to Him by abandoning evil influences. May you learn to discern the Holy Spirit's voice. Daily, surrender to His guidance and let Him use you for His glory!

Double Shot

1. Where am I tempted to rely on appearance or routine instead of a genuine relationship with Jesus?

2. What practices help me stay sensitive to the Holy Spirit's voice so my ministry flows from His leading, not my effort?

3. What needs to be surrendered so God can work through me with integrity and power?

Time For Prayer
Take a moment and communicate with God.

"For you have brought these men here who are not temple robbers or blasphemers of our goddess." vs 37

Who are you when no one seems to be looking? Does it matter if your private self is different than your public self?

Paul's companions found themselves in a very public setting which was sure unsettling. What was it that God used to deliver them from such a large crowd? Their integrity! The city clerk mentioned the fact that the men had done nothing immoral, irresponsible, or sinful against their goddess Artemis. The clerk's recognition of their character speaks volumes about the lives of Gaius and Aristarchus. They had learned valuable lessons from Paul during their time together. Paul's courage is reflected in them. Their godly integrity was obvious and observable by all. Who you are in private and in public matters. What actions can you take to tighten the gap between the public and private you? Would the clerk have been able to say the same of you? Ask God to shape your life so your public and private lives align in Christ Jesus.

Double Shot

1. What gaps exist between my private life and my public life, and what needs to change for those to align in Christ?

2. Who sees my character up close, and what would they honestly say about the way I live?

3. What habits or choices can strengthen integrity so my life speaks for Christ even when I am not being watched?

Time For Prayer
Take a moment and communicate with God.

Cup 59
Acts 20:7-12

"On the first day of the week, we assembled to break bread." vs 7a

Gathering with like-minded believers is vital to our growth as disciples, grounded in the fellowship we share and the conviction we gain spiritually. The early believers devoted much of their time to hearing Paul teach because they recognized the benefit. They experienced such a benefit when Eutychus fell out of the window and was revived by Paul. Eutychus not only reveals how God works physically among us but how He longs to spiritually renew us when we seek Him. God rewards those faithfully seeking Him. A band of men who hunt will not only hunt together, but will spend money and time to develop a hunting camp from which to gather and actively hunt. We are no different, or should be no different. If we are willing to devote time and effort to secular connections, how much more should we invest our time, talents, money, and attention to God's family? When we gather, God willingly strengthens and renews us just as He gave life back to Eutychus.

Double Shot

1. How committed am I to gathering with believers, and what does that commitment reveal about my spiritual priorities?

2. Where have I settled for secular community while neglecting the kind of fellowship God uses to renew me?

3. How can I invest my time, energy, and resources more intentionally in the life of the church?

Time For Prayer
Take a moment and communicate with God.

Cup 60
Acts 20:13-38

"But I consider my life of no value to myself; my purpose is to finish my course and the ministry I received from the Lord Jesus, to testify to the gospel of God's grace." vs 24

Paul is embarking on a difficult journey. He spends time with familiar friends in Ephesus. During that time he imparts one last message of encouragement. Paul calls his friends to live out the hope of Jesus as they surrender to the will of God. Though serving God can include times of difficulty, we can have the mindset of Paul. The mind set of Paul is clear as he states, "I consider my life of no value to myself"(v 24a). His focus was on completing the ministry entrusted to his care. He warns his friends of false teachers who can disrupt their fellowship once he has departed. His deepest concern was they remain faithful to the message of the Gospel. View your life as secondary in comparison to the work of God's Kingdom. Just as Paul poured out his life, parents make great sacrifices to ensure their children are given the chance to grow up and become adults. Are you similarly focused on the work of God in the world? Commit yourself fully to God's grace, finishing the work He has given you with faithfulness, to His honor and glory.

Double Shot

1. What part of my life am I still treating as more valuable than the work God has given me?

2. Where do I need to realign my focus so that faithfulness in God's mission becomes the priority again?

3. What step of obedience would help me finish the course God has placed before me with greater faithfulness?

Time For Prayer
Take a moment and communicate with God.

Cup 61
Acts 21:1-36

"Since he would not be persuaded, we said no more except, "The Lord's will be done." vs14

One of the most difficult prayers we may utter models Jesus' prayer in the garden, "Lord, let Your will be done." Pursuing the greater purpose of God in your life is a selfless act. Paul knew difficulties were ahead as he set his heart and mind to advance the Kingdom of God. The only way forward was to remain resolute in heart and surrendered to God's will. He expressed this conviction when he said in verse 13, "I am ready not only to be bound but also to die...for the name of the Lord Jesus." Friends of Paul joined him in praying in verse 14, "The Lord's will be done." Though not easy, you can pray the same, but you must be prepared to obediently follow the prompting of the Holy Spirit. You can face tremendous circumstances like the angry mob Paul faced in the Temple of Jerusalem, when you have committed to God's will. You will be bolstered internally by the Holy Spirit to face both good and bad from following the will of God. Meditate on the seriousness of praying such a prayer. Can you trust God enough to pray for His will? Allow God's faithfulness to guide you to surrender as you pray.

Double Shot

1. When you pray for God's will to be done, what fears or hesitations rise within your heart, and how can you surrender them to the Holy Spirit?

2. In what current situation do you sense God calling you to trust Him beyond what feels comfortable?

3. How might remembering God's past faithfulness strengthen your resolve to walk obediently into His will today?

Time For Prayer
Take a moment and communicate with God.

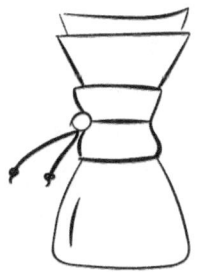

Cup 62
Acts 21:37-22:29

"He said to me, 'I am Jesus of Nazareth, the one you are persecuting." vs 8b

Responses to the Good News of Jesus Christ are varied. Some individuals are open to the Gospel while others are a bit more resistant. Paul faced the latter while visiting Jerusalem. Though the situation seemed to be chaotic, Paul was given an opportunity to address the angry mob clamoring for his demise. He did not shout back in anger, he simply pointed to his faith relationship with Jesus. What made the greatest impact in his life was his encounter with Jesus, "Saul, Saul, why are you persecuting me?"(Acts 22:7) Testimony is powerful in two directions. First, your testimony is your strength as you face difficulties. You can remain faithful as you recall how Jesus transformed your life. Second, your testimony testifies to the saving power of Jesus' sacrifice on the cross. Personal testimonies personalize the Gospel, making the love of Jesus real. Let Paul's story remind you of your own encounter with Jesus. How can your relationship with God help you remain calm and Christlike as you share Jesus with others? Ask God to show you someone who needs to hear your story and be ready to share it.

Double Shot

1. How does recalling your personal encounter with Jesus help you remain calm and Christlike when others push back against your faith?

2. Who in your life needs to hear the simplicity of your story, and how can you be sensitive to the Spirit's prompting to share it?

3. When resistance arises, how can you anchor yourself again in the transforming work Jesus has already done in you?

Time For Prayer
Take a moment and communicate with God.

Cup 63
Acts 22:30-23:11

The following night, the Lord stood by him and said, "Have courage! For as you have testified about me in Jerusalem, so it is necessary for you to testify in Rome." vs 11

The scene is one of chaos. Not on Paul's part but on the part of the religious leaders. Paul related the Gospel of Jesus Christ and the opponents of Jesus strongly reacted. How would Paul respond? As the accusations flew his direction, he quietly, yet firmly, stood his ground for the Gospel. The scene grew even more chaotic when the high priest gave the command to strike him on the mouth. Paul continued to remain calm in the midst of the fury and anger being hurled at him. How did Paul find the internal fortitude to remain calm? The faithfulness of God. God is faithful to His servants. He did not really know how this particular situation would play out, but he did depend on the faithfulness of God to carry him through. Night comes and God reaffirms His plans for Paul to bear witness in Rome. You can remain calm when you encounter chaos in sharing the Gospel too. Reflect on the faithfulness of God. How can you find strength to remain calm when a person you are sharing with responds with anger?

Double Shot

1. When chaos surrounds you, what truths about God's faithfulness can you cling to so you remain steady rather than shaken?

2. How can you prepare your heart in advance for moments when someone reacts harshly to the Gospel you share?

3. Where in your life do you need to hear the Lord whisper again, "Have courage," and trust that He is standing by you?

Time For Prayer
Take a moment and communicate with God.

"...I am glad to offer my defense in what concerns me." 24:10b

A whirlwind of activity takes place and sweeps Paul along rather quickly. He escapes a plot against his life, he is whisked along at night to avoid detection, and now he is in Caesarea before the governor. How would Paul respond facing accusations of being an agitator? Would he cave to the pressure and try to reverse course? No, he did not. Paul didn't back down at all. He welcomed the opportunity to defend his faith in Jesus Christ. He took advantage of his situation to spread the Good News. You might be wondering the same about yourself. Would you reconsider and back down about your message of Jesus, or would you have the courage of Paul to share your faith? You should always be ready to give a defense for the faith within you. You can follow in the footsteps of Paul and find the strength of the Holy Spirit within and share what you know to be true. Could you say like Paul, "I am glad to offer my defense."(24:10)?

Double Shot

1. What situations in your life feel like pressure trying to silence your witness, and how can you respond with Paul's confidence rather than retreat?

2. How can you posture your heart to be "glad to offer a defense" of your faith when God opens an unexpected door?

3. Where might the Holy Spirit be inviting you to speak truth boldly instead of shrinking back for fear of opposition?

Time For Prayer
Take a moment and communicate with God.

Cup 65
Acts 24:22-25:27

"Neither against the Jewish law, not against the temple, nor against Caesar have I sinned in any way" v. 25:7

Having a clear conscience leads to strength under pressure when it concerns our witness. Paul was not guilty of any crime which led to having a clear path to present the Gospel in the best light. Like Paul, you can have an easier time sharing the Good News when people observe you are a person of integrity. Sharing is a lot like driving down the street. Your drive is easier when you do not have to deal with deep pot holes or barricades blocking the road. Your life's decisions are the potential pot holes or barricades that can hinder or help your sharing efforts. Paul refers to the clear path ahead when he notes, "neither against the Jewish law...the temple...nor against Caesar have I sinned."(25:7) Are you able to claim a similar claim as Paul's? Take a moment and reflect on your life in the past few weeks. Which personal actions would hinder your sharing the Gospel of Jesus with a person in your life? What actions would enhance or make your sharing easier? Ask God to strengthen you to make wise life choices thereby giving the Holy Spirit a greater opportunity to use you to reach others.

Double Shot

1. What recent choices or habits might create "potholes" that complicate your ability to share Jesus with others, and how can you repair them?

2. What actions from the past few weeks reflect Christ well and make the road smoother for Gospel conversations?

3. How can you invite the Holy Spirit to strengthen your integrity so your life becomes a clear pathway for the Good News?

Time For Prayer
Take a moment and communicate with God.

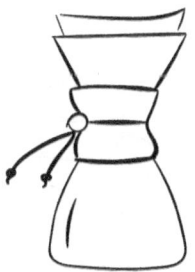

Cup 66
Acts 26:1-32

"I consider myself fortunate, that it is before you King Agrippa, I am to make my defense..." vs2

How do you view sharing your faith with others? Paul considered it an honor to have the opportunity to share his testimony with King Agrippa. His desire was for the message of Jesus to impact everyone who was listening to his story. Jesus made such a difference in Paul's life that evangelism became natural. As a result, the Holy Spirit was able to use his testimony to challenge King Agrippa. Though he rejects the moving of the Holy Spirit, his response draws out Paul's passion. He replies, "...not only you but all who listen to me today might become as I am..."(v. 29). Paul considered it an honor to be able to invite others to a faith relationship. Can you be like Paul? You can make a great impact on the people who are in your life. Do you consider it an honor to be able to share your faith with those in your life? Reflect upon your view of sharing your faith. If you have lost your passion for Jesus, ask God to renew your heart. Once you have regained your passion, allow it to drive your efforts to share.

Double Shot

1. How do you honestly view the privilege of sharing your faith, and what might need to shift in your heart to see it as an honor?

2. Where have you lost passion for Jesus, and what would it look like for you to ask God to renew that fire?

3. Who in your life might be impacted if you approached evangelism with the same joy and expectancy Paul displayed before Agrippa?

Time For Prayer
Take a moment and communicate with God.

Cup 67
Acts 27:1-44

"So take courage, men, because I believe God that it will be just the way it was told to me" v. 25

Paul was on a dangerous journey as a prisoner to Rome, but being in the will of God provided him tremendous courage to face the unknown along the way. Though he faced difficulty, he inspired others around him to trust in Jesus. Acts 27:20 shares the difficulty Paul encountered, "For many days neither sun nor stars appeared, and the severe storm kept raging". While the storm raged, God promised Paul protection for every one onboard. Paul then offered God's words of encouragement to the men as they faced the storm. He called his shipmates to trust in the providence of God. God's faithfulness is recorded in verse 44, "In this way, everyone safely reached the shore." Paul's trust in Jesus provided a contagious courage. The life of a disciple is not to be lived in isolation from others. You are called to live out your faith as you go through all circumstances you may encounter. You can impact others in positive ways just as Paul's life had a positive influence. Who could benefit from your courage? Reach out today.

Double Shot

1. What storm are you facing right now, and how can God's promises steady your heart so you can offer courage to those around you?

2. Who in your life needs to borrow your faith until they rediscover their own courage in Jesus?

3. How can you intentionally live your faith publicly this week so others are strengthened by your trust in God's providence?

Time For Prayer
Take a moment and communicate with God.

Cup 68
Acts 28:1-10

"They expected that he would begin to swell up or suddenly drop dead." vs 6

Paul's life never lacked excitement as observed in the Book of Acts. Acts 28:3 relates another moment when life took a dramatic turn, a snake came out of the fire and grabbed ahold of his hand? What did Paul think as he shook the snake off into the fire? Those watching this unfold waited for him to fall over dead. Nope, Paul continued as if nothing had happened. The confidence in God's promise continued to be his. Because of what happened, they considered Paul a god. Not to take glory from God, Paul directed their attention to the power of God to heal all. God gave Paul the opportunity to not only heal, but to share the Good News through his circumstances. Similarly, your life can be tough, but you can be used by the Holy Spirit even in the midst of trying times. Take encouragement from Paul's courage to shake the snake off, shake off the temptation to withdraw and stand tall as you walk in the encouragement of the Holy Spirit. Seek opportunities to share with those who are watching, even if they think it is over for you.

Double Shot

1. What "snake bites" in your life tempt you to withdraw, and how can you shake them off and stand firm in the Spirit's encouragement?

2. Who is watching your response to hardship, and how might God use your resilience to point them toward His power?

3. How can you stay attentive to the opportunities God gives you to share Jesus even in seasons when life feels unfair or overwhelming?

Time For Prayer
Take a moment and communicate with God.

Cup 69
Acts 28:11-22

"When Paul saw them, he thanked God and took courage." vs. 15

If the Book of Acts conveys anything else about Paul, his love for others shone brightly. Everywhere Paul went, he discovered individuals in need of God's saving grace. His love for all undergirded a passion to share the Good News of Jesus so others would not perish in their sins. The love he poured out was reciprocated many times over and when Paul arrived in Rome, many who had heard of his mission came to meet and greet him. Verse 15 relays just how much Paul needed this expression of love. "He thanked God and took courage" reveals he needed to be loved as well as to love. From Jerusalem, to Malta, and now in Rome, the journey had been long and dangerous. Getting to Rome was a time of relief and he needed renewal. Part of that renewal came by an expression of love from others. Do not underestimate the need for others to invest in you. Like Paul, you need to love others but you need to take time to relish the love of others. Take a moment and list the people you cherish and love. Thank God for them and reflect how they express their love back to you. Let the Holy Spirit renew your heart as you give glory to God for the relationships you enjoy.

Double Shot

1. Who has poured love and encouragement into your life lately, and how can you pause to thank God for their presence?

2. In what ways do you need spiritual renewal, and how can receiving the love of others help restore your heart?

3. How can you be intentional this week in both giving love and allowing yourself to be loved so the Holy Spirit can refresh your soul

Time For Prayer
Take a moment and communicate with God.

Cup 70
Acts 28:23-31

"Paul stayed two whole years in his own rented house. And he welcomed all who visited him." vs 30

We come to the end of the journey of the heroes we have encountered. The story does not really end, but pauses a moment to reflect upon the greatness of God. What God started in Acts 1:8 continues as the curtain closes with Paul "proclaiming the kingdom of God and teaching about the Lord Jesus Christ with all boldness and without hindrance."(v. 321) Stephen stood firm and was martyred. Phillip ran and shared with a chariot riding eunuch. Peter, because of his vision, visited with Cornelius. Paul obediently went to Jerusalem in order to be sent to Rome. His journey was not an easy endeavor, but he persevered and God was demonstrated to be faithful. The story of the Book of Acts really is not about the men and women we consider the heroes of our faith, but is about the God who was faithful. Your life is not to be about you either. You are to point all who observe your life to the faithfulness of Jesus Christ of Nazareth. What changes in your life could help those who peer into your life see, not you, but God?

Double Shot

1. How can I shift my perspective to view the events and struggles in my life less as personal battles and more as opportunities to reflect God's faithfulness to those around me?

2. What are some practical ways I can live with boldness, like the heroes in Acts, so that those observing my life would see more of God's work in me than my own accomplishments or struggles?

3. In what areas of my life can I surrender control and trust God more fully, allowing Him to use me as a vessel for His kingdom rather than focusing on my own plans or comfort?

Time For Prayer
Take a moment and communicate with God.

Closing Remarks

Thank you for allowing me to share my thoughts as we have walked together through Dr. Luke's inspiring Book of Acts. My prayer is that, as we reach this final page, you have drawn closer to our Lord Jesus Christ. May you be encouraged by the heroes of our faith and strengthened to remain faithful to Him in every season of life.

Do not let the lessons found in these chapters remain only on the pages of this book. Let them sink deeply into your heart, challenge your daily walk, and transform the way you live.

May God bless you richly through our Lord and Savior, Jesus Christ. Amen.

ALL FOR CHRIST!

Dr. Raymond GRABERT

Author Bio

Dr. Raymond Grabert has been a pastor for over 30 years. Currently, he serves as pastor of Big Ridge Baptist Church, D'Iberville, MS. His native state is Louisiana where he met and married his wife of 36 years. Educated at New Orleans Baptist Theological Seminary, he holds the B.G.S, M.DIV., and D.MIN. Degrees.